Bread of the Imagined

Bilingual Press/Editorial Bilingüe

General Editor
Gary D. Keller

Managing Editor
Karen S. Van Hooft

Associate Editor
Ann M. Waggoner

Assistant Editor
Linda St. George Thurston

Editorial Consultant
Jennifer Hartfield Prochnow

Editorial Board
Juan Goytisolo
Francisco Jiménez
Eduardo Rivera
Severo Sarduy
Mario Vargas Llosa

Address:
Bilingual Review/Press
Hispanic Research Center
Arizona State University
Tempe, Arizona 85287
(602) 965-3867

Bread of the Imagined

Ricardo Pau-Llosa

Bilingual Press/Editorial Bilingüe
TEMPE, ARIZONA

ISBN 0-927534-16-9

Library of Congress Cataloging-in-Publication Data

Pau-Llosa, Ricardo.
    Bread of the imagined / by Ricardo Pau-Llosa.
        p.   cm.
    ISBN 0-927534-16-9 (pbk.)
    I. Title.
    PS3566.A82614B7   1991
    811'.54—dc20   91-11914
                                                  CIP

PRINTED IN THE UNITED STATES OF AMERICA

Cover design by Kerry Curtis
Front cover painting "En la espera" by Rafael Soriano
Back cover photo by Mario Algaze

Acknowledgments

Grateful acknowledgment is given to the following publications and organizations for permission to reprint some of the poems appearing in this collection:

Bilingual Review/Press, for "Caryatides," in *Hispanics in the United States: An Anthology of Creative Literature*, eds. Gary D. Keller & Francisco Jiménez (Ypsilanti, MI: Bilingual Press, 1980).
The Devil's Millhopper, for "The Burial of the Elephant at Cremona," in Vol. 7, No. 2 (Fall 1982), and "Smoke" (1990).
The Missouri Review, for "Swirling Lines," in Vol. 7, No. 3 (1984).
The Fiddlehead, for "Exile," in No. 139 (Spring 1984).
Kayak, for "Foreign Language," in No. 64 (May 1984).
Beloit Poetry Journal, for "The Inventors," in Vol. 35, No. 1 (Fall 1984).
Cedarmere Review, for "Freedom as Etymology," in No. 1 (Fall 1985).
Agni Review, for "Brooms," in No. 22 (1985).
Carolina Quarterly, for "Battlefields," in Vol. 38, No. 1 (Fall 1985).
Black Warrior Review, for "What is a Face?" and "The Room," in Vol. 12 (Fall 1985).

(Acknowledgments continue on next page.)

Acknowledgments *(continued)*

The Carrell, for "Aquarium," in Vol. 23 (1985).

Albatross, for "Trees and Transformations," in Vol. 1, No. 2 (1986).

The American Poetry Review, for "Fog's Edge," in Vol. 16, No. 4 (July/August 1987).

Denver Quarterly, for "The Island of Mirrors," in Vol. 21, No. 3 (Winter 1987) and "The Intruder," in Vol. 23, Nos. 3/4 (Winter & Spring 1989).

Linden Lane Magazine, for "Seals," "The Beauty of Treason," and "Point Blank: The Footbridge," in Vol. VII, No. 1 (Jan./March 1988).

Downtown (New York City), for "Nude Man Bending into a Mirror," "Little Dog," "The Flight of the Labyrinth Maker's Son," "Articles of Childhood," "The Metaphor of Menace," and "Fly," in No. 175 (Dec. 20-27, 1989).

Massachusetts Review, for "Dart," in Vol. 31, No. 4 (Fall 1990).

Tampa Review, for "Orchids" and "Key Biscayne," in No. 3 (Fall 1990).

Contents

For my mother, María Llosa

A Voice for an Inarticulate Hunger:
Ricardo Pau-Llosa's *Bread of the Imagined*

Dionisio D. Martínez

> Selves want to be wholes, but have lately also taken to longing to be parts.
>
> —Allan Bloom, *The Closing of the American Mind*

The Hazards of an Either/Or World

An Us-and-Them attitude prevails in North America. Glendale, California, was a predominantly white, Anglo-Saxon and largely Presbyterian city in the early seventies. It was difficult for the Anglo-Saxon children to distinguish between the various ethnic groups that were becoming a part of our student body in junior high school. But children can grow up and out of this limited thinking. What frightens me, remembering those days, is that most school administrators and teachers shared the students' indiscriminate grouping of everyone who came from that vague Elsewhere, otherwise known as the rest of the world.

As a member of the Them group, I was asked to help new Spanish-speaking students. Cuban, Argentinian, and Mexican children would arrive, and I would take them from class to class, show them around the school, and generally make them feel comfortable in their new country. This was a relatively simple assignment until a girl from Greece arrived. "She doesn't speak English," an administrator told me. "I'm sure you can be her interpreter."

Just this week, at the local public library, I found this subject card:

HISPANO

SEE

MEXICAN

Even this close to the twenty-first century, the Us-and-Them attitude is alive and well in the United States. The Us live somewhere north of Mexico and south of Canada. The Them live in that

vague Elsewhere, otherwise known as the rest of the world. The
Them can be of any nationality, race, or creed.

It is the synthesis of Us and Them that Ricardo Pau-Llosa has
mastered for more than a decade. Wendell Berry, writing about
regionalism, refers to Huck Finn's voice as one "governed always
by a need to flow, to move outward."[1] Pau-Llosa has achieved this
flow in *Bread of the Imagined.*

Guillermo Cabrera Infante opens his novel *Tres Tristes Tigres*
by warning the reader that the work is written in Cuban. Mark
Twain's characters sound somewhat incomprehensible at times
when translated into Spanish. Even García Lorca's poems, with all
their music, occasionally sound flat in English. And it is not so
much a technical problem as it is one of regionalism. Twain must
sound just as dissonant to Australians as some passages from
García Lorca's work sound to Cubans. There is an inherent music
in every region. It is a music that fades with distance: the farther it
travels, the more irrelevant its details become. It is not only the
North American who is guilty of grouping the rest of the world
into a single category; regionalism makes everyone guilty.

Unlike other Hispanics of his generation, Pau-Llosa is a poet
whose region has become more than just North America with a
Creole accent. His poems are linked simultaneously by a sense of
security and a sense of transition. For many Cubans, after all, exile
is a temporary condition. Elías Miguel Muñoz writes of the island
as seen by the exile:

> La isla es mito, pero también historia. Se esconde en
> una canción, en una fantasía. Pero también la vemos en
> los rostros de los recién llegados, en nuestros propios
> rostros, en las cartas de los familiares que todavía nos
> escriben. La isla está en Miami; sus olores, su clima, su
> acento han sido conservados en una cápsula del tiempo.
> La verdadera isla, el "cocodrilo", es tan inescapable
> como inasequible. La patria es la marca, la identidad
> perdida. El misterio.[2]

There is, however, in this world within the world, yet another
world. It is here that Pau-Llosa lets his poems root themselves. The
first stanza of the poem that opens *Bread of the Imagined* illustrates
the result:

> The dream where land
> breaks like surf
> cannot be dreamt.
> Such a dream would pull
> the anchor from the heart
> and set the world adrift
> like a plague ship,
> the rats turning into words.

Not wanting to "set the world adrift" is a common concern among Cuban writers of Pau-Llosa's generation. Their exile is not difficult to define. It began with a cataclysmic change in their native island on New Year's Day, 1959. Pau-Llosa carries the historical baggage that leaps now and then from one of his poems. But he grew up and matured surrounded by the tradition of Whitman, Williams, Eliot, and others that sculpted this poetry we call American.

He embraced his new models and his new language, but his rich tradition lingered and this has made his region accessible to at least two cultures. All poetry, by one definition or another, is regional, but when your region takes on the dimensions of Pau-Llosa's world, hardly anyone or anything escapes it. At times the poetry is aggressive, overpowering, almost violent.

The first section of the book has the intensity, vigor, and stamina of a long distance runner. But like a good runner, it knows how to pace itself: though exile is the recurrent theme, its aggressiveness gives in to the tranquility of all temporary conditions. Like the Doppler effect, it gains momentum, reaches its climax, and levels off again.

At the end of each scream is a voice of reason:

> Then we would have made the hours pure
> with the hand, the kiss, the word.

Like Echo's, this calm voice always has the last word. But unlike the mythological character, it doesn't think of this as a curse. Pau-Llosa's voice has come to terms with its new language and its new condition.

The Failure of Denial

A good tradition must come equipped with myths—plenty of them. "A great color need not be ambiguous," declares the opening line of the second section's title poem. In Pau-Llosa's poetry, history and myth steer clear of ambiguity. And in a seemingly effortless manner, he makes of these elements a single current that flows toward the present:

> This bar is an aquarium
> with an aquarium for a heart.

Somehow, the commonplace takes on the dimensions of the past. Poetry has the power of reminding both writer and reader of things read and heard as well as of things never read or heard.[3] "Aquarium" is both trivial and historically significant, both current and ancient. The Catholic symbolism of the fish cannot be avoided. Every line, every word is a reminder of something. Formality permeates the syntax of this and other poems: each sentence unwinds with the methodical craftsmanship of the more narrative poems of John Ashbery and other ground-breaking North American poets who in one form or another have given color to Pau-Llosa's voice. And all along, there is the underlying, unmistakable presence of the past. The symbolic and literal fish of his childhood swim in his aquarium.

This connection with the past is the line of demarcation between Pau-Llosa and many of his Anglo-Saxon contemporaries with whom he shares so much. North American poets born in the fifties have grown up with the myths of Marilyn Monroe, James Dean, and Elvis. Pau-Llosa had all of those icons, but he also had a rich tradition in which pop culture played a rather insignificant role. This clash has been, and still is, the catalyst for the voice that has been growing inside him all these years:

> He was from another country,
> ambassador, discreet, often in love.
> He had learned the music of the court
> and found it better than that of his own
> land, which he was now forgetting.

But the poet never really forgets. This is about "the beauty of treason," and about how the exile is a pragmatic yet romantic creature. There is, in this entire section of the book, a sense not only of the author coming to terms with history and with his present condition, but also a sense of the modern world coming to terms with a history it has unsuccessfully tried to deny.

Pau-Llosa on Pau-Llosa

It is when he consciously writes about others, particularly artists, that Pau-Llosa is truly autobiographical and perhaps more vulnerable and self-revealing than he might be when dealing with other subjects. Perhaps because he doesn't want to speak for the visual artists, Pau-Llosa finds pieces of himself, as if he were finding pieces of a shattered mirror, when looking at these works.

Like the bulk of his work, his poems on art refuse to follow linear thought. Eventually everything returns to the source.

When Stephen Dobyns wrote *The Balthus Poems* he was working from a distance, both chronologically and geographically. Pau-Llosa, however, is very close to his subjects. Like Dobyns, he has tried to avoid a literal reading of the works that sparked the poems. Like Dobyns, he has succeeded. It is the question of proximity that makes Pau-Llosa's poems in the third section of *Bread of the Imagined* unique.

In the world of art criticism, the name Ricardo Pau-Llosa has been seen and heard for years, and is very well respected. He has written:

> The exile knows his place, and that place is the imagi-
> nation. Modernism is a culture of the imagination more
> so than that of any previous era, because modernism is a
> culture of exiles. Twentieth century Cuba offers a prime
> example of this phenomenon.[4]

The Cuban poet in exile steps back and tries to write objectively about the visual arts created by his countrymen and other Hispanics. Soon though, the linear thought employed in referring to the subject breaks off or reaches a wall from which it ricochets. And this, precisely, is what happens in this section of the book. The art critic disappears in these poems. What we hear is the voice of a man who loves art for its own sake and suddenly finds himself alone in a gallery or a museum, talking to himself.

These are Pau-Llosa's friends, their images are his obsessions. In these lines we learn more about the poet than about the artists on whose works the poems are based. It is as though he were writing an autobiography in the third person. Some claim that much of the power of nineteenth century realism has nothing to do with the talent of the artists; that each viewer's interpretation (and all the sentiments attached to that interpretation) is the real power of the visual arts from the last century.[5] Some would argue that contemporary art is no different. Even photographs, which sometimes try desperately to mirror reality, are "haunted by tacit imperatives of taste and conscience,"[6] according to Susan Sontag.

Because Western culture forces us to interpret and draw our own conclusions from the visual arts, Pau-Llosa's poems about contemporary Hispanic artists not only tell us about the poet but about us all. They remind us of our need for images, of how we sooner or later become the images that surround us. In his poem "Brooms," after a photograph by Mario Algaze, the inanimate objects gradually acquire human traits:

> This bouquet of brooms will fall apart
> that one by one they might claim
> the territory of some function
> in each house on the village street.

Elsewhere, obsessions recur:

> In the myth of conflict, doubt sustains.
> The winner, disguised in calculations,
> trembles before the prey.

One would not expect most contemporary, non-Cuban Hispanic writers to speak of "the myth of conflict," but Pau-Llosa's work, being one of synthesis, does not confront or provoke. As long as exile is a temporary condition, confrontation is not necessary. The poems in this section are variations on the life of a man who at times lives vicariously through the colors and textures of the visual arts he so much admires.

There are symbols within symbols, much like Poe's "dream within a dream":

> The sharpened symbols and the table
> come upon him like panthers rising
> from a dart's dream. The flesh
> imagines, the flesh holds mirrors
> to eyes that swim out to sea
> and mark a horizon in each stroke
> as the frames in a movie
> mark the destinies of light.

The underlying current running through Hispanic American art is a sense of life as stage, something Pau-Llosa is well aware of:

> In the poetics of [Paul] Sierra, the scenario is itself, and as such, the scenario impels the viewer into a direct and dramatic interaction with what is represented. The power of Sierra's painting lies in his ability to draw the spectator into the unsettling passions of his world.[7]

Pau-Llosa's world, like Sierra's, has certain unsettling passions in the midst of an otherwise symmetrical structure. One reconciliatory measure between the artist and the world is an attempt to strike a balance between those unsettling passions and the other end of the emotional/subconscious spectrum. Pau-Llosa's meeting with the world takes place at the point where he makes sense of all the symbols, the subtleties, the blurred images. As he points out in the poem "White Water,"

> In the painting, the houses and trees
> are not shattered or drowned but gathered
> and laid, like offerings,
> at the feet of blind pillars.

This sense of logic and sanity in the midst of chaos and disaster is one of the first lessons one learns in a temporary exile.

The Center of the Ellipse

Bread of the Imagined begins with, but goes beyond, Wittgenstein's object-designation theory of meaning[8] in which the Austrian-born philosopher argues that one must know to what every single word in a sentence refers in order to understand its factual import. But even Wittgenstein allows for the unexplained, the mystic. He never completely discards the element of chance. Decades later, Richard Hugo tells us that "the poem is always in your hometown, but you have a better chance of finding it in another."[9] His explanation is a rather simple one: it is easier to write about that which is distant because we know too much about our own town and are too emotionally attached to it. The one you build from scratch in your mind becomes your "triggering town," the source of your poem. Pau-Llosa's generation is searching for something between exact language, on the one hand and, on the other, the triggering town in which the ultimate poem resides beyond and in spite of language.

The book's final section lives up to its title. The swirling lines take us out of our triggering towns and bring us back. It is a kinetic exercise, an ellipse of words in search of a center. The poet and the exile both know their place: it is one and the same place. This knowledge allows the poet to explore. That is not to say that what emerges is merely exploratory poetry, but there is a strong element of that in the closing section. "What is a Face?" ranks among the most exquisitely executed exploratory poems published in North American literary journals in the 1980s. The ellipse is in motion throughout the entire work:

> A face is a storm-felled branch,
> and any kind of clothes especially armor
> and lace, and a postcard, but it can never be
> punctuation or anything determined by chance
> like the paths of wind-blown newspapers.

It is this questioning, this obsession with chance that gives these last poems coherence. At first there are only fractions, but the whole emerges with a more careful reading. One whole becomes a fraction of a larger whole, and so on. There is continuity in this, a feeling of eternity of which language is quite often, if not always, the root:

> Every object is a room
> you walk words into.
> Take an apple, its windows peeling.
> In your hands the apple's
> door opens a crack
> and the words barge through
> like salesmen confident of a kill.

When you've traveled and explored as much as Ricardo Pau-Llosa has traveled and explored, you begin to redefine *regionalism* in broader and broader terms. Eventually, every corner of the world is home and every town triggers a poem that rings with confidence.

Bread as Metaphor

In 1973 Orlando Rodríguez Sardiñas published what would become the definitive anthology of contemporary Cuban poetry written since the 1959 revolution. (Poetry written in Spanish—on the island and in exile.) Rodríguez Sardiñas points out in his introduction that 1960 marks the beginning of a series of events with serious and lasting repercussions:

> A partir de 1960 muchos de los jóvenes poetas que de una manera decidida colaboraron con los ideales de la Revolución, se van defraudando ante el impacto de los acontecimientos; otros, sin embargo, parecen ignorar el problema o adherirse a su causa. El tajo revolucionario va a separar ideológicamente primero y geográfica- mente después a toda una generación que se disponía a dar un paso al frente al llamado nacional, tanto en el aspecto cívico como en el literario.[10]

The youngest poet in the anthology by Rodríguez Sardiñas is nearly a decade older than Pau-Llosa, whose generation emerged and matured in exile, long after the intellectual community became disillusioned with Castro.[11] This generation of transi- tional writers[12] works mostly with what is simultaneously a for- eign and familiar tongue. No crystal ball prepared us for the emergence of these people caught between two cultures.

Ricardo Pau-Llosa's first book, *Sorting Metaphors*, winner of the 1983 Anhinga Prize for Poetry, was one of the first collections

by Cubans who remembered just enough of home yet felt at home
in exile. In these poems Pau-Llosa began what would become a
loyal and almost obsessive relationship with language:

> The tongue of the rebel god is the anaconda,
> so says the tribal legend, cut from his mouth
> before words that carried secrets
> which make gods gods could rise
> to the ears of men.[13]

All the gears that make Pau-Llosa's poetry unique had been set
in motion. All the myths, fears, all the history, had begun to
appear. The title poem is a tightrope walk between a cold aesthetic
eye and unabashed nostalgia. Somehow, the speaker successfully
walks the length of the rope:

> Only a map is left of that Havana,
> major buildings towering
> pencil marks on a grid,
> half the city fitting under my spread hand
> moving back from P-K4, lightly
> arched fingers, the opponent's
> intense sight and clicking of his time . . .[14]

Even at that age (he was in his early twenties), his craftsman-
ship was evident; one could follow him as he transformed some-
thing as insignificant as fingers on a map into a ritual rich with
tropes, which he considered "the software of consciousness."[15] His
poetry, in those days, pivoted around metaphors. Narration would
come with *Bread of the Imagined*. He worked vigorously, even
then, with the visual arts—curating exhibitions and writing criti-
cism (primarily on contemporary Latin American artists)—but in
his poetry, imagery always followed ideas; the metaphors always
had something solid on which to lean. And sound would always
play an indispensable role. He felt that "one of the satisfactions of
writing in English is the ample sonorous range of that language,
the result of its lexical diversity and richness."[16]

Having gathered the raw materials, Pau-Llosa was now ready
to give life to his blueprints, building beyond metaphors, carefully
exploring each new angle and each new space he encountered on

the way to *Bread of the Imagined*—an exploration that continues to this day.

The Either/Or World, Revisited

In the last book of *The Republic*, Socrates takes on the poets. It would be fair, he claims, to ask Homer, "What city was goverened better because of you?"[17] If Homer's answer is "None," Socrates is convinced, the poet is nothing more than an imitator and a manufacturer of images.[18] This makes the poet and his vocation rather useless in the philosopher's eyes. What good, after all, is someone who can give us an imitation of the truth but not the truth itself? Poetry, seen this way, is aesthetic baggage with no substance. Academia, and society in general, will sing its praises, but just like the political exile, the poet must know his or her place.

The Cuban American poet carries a double burden. An exaggerated and perhaps excessively romantic image of the exiled Cuban, particularly the Miami Cuban, has been perpetuated by writers such as Joan Didion. In her book *Miami,*[19] Didion tells us repeatedly that Anglos don't understand Cuban culture, but she does so with the coldness of those Anglos to whom she refers. There is, in her book and in our society at large, a popular view of Cubans and other Hispanics as exclusively political creatures. Hispanic art is far too often viewed in a strictly political context by Anglos. The Cuban writer of Pau-Llosa's generation is frequently excluded from both ends of the literary spectrum. Neither the older Cuban writers nor the Anglo writers and publishers can find a label for a young Cuban who is writing almost exclusively in English.[20] But it is not so much a matter of discrimination as it is an inability—by both the Anglo and Hispanic communities—to understand this kind of assimilation, this generation's grasp of both cultures. It is a new sensibility and a new phenomenon.

It was so much easier when everything was either Us or Them: the good old days of Desi Arnaz singing "Babalú" on our black and white TV sets; the days of flights from Miami to Havana and a taxi from the airport to the Tropicana; days in Varadero Beach, nights by the Malecón, and a good rest in a luxurious room at the Habana Hilton. It was so much easier. Cubans were exotic. Cubans were distant. North America, comfortable with that image of Cubans, could sleep with its windows open and its doors unlocked because

there was no danger of waking at four in the morning, multicultur-
alism tapping the sleeper on the shoulder.

In 1959 the long sleep ended and the danger began. The Tropi-
cana, Varadero, and the Malecón would be out of North America's
reach. The Habana Hilton would become the Habana Libre.
Cubans would begin to arrive in the United States (a temporary
stop for Cubans, a potentially dangerous intrusion as far as some
North Americans were concerned). Gradually, this wave of exiles
would become politically and financially powerful. By the late
seventies, the writing was not only on the wall, but on the bumper
stickers:

WILL THE LAST AMERICAN TO LEAVE MIAMI
PLEASE BRING THE FLAG

Cubans were no longer exotic, no longer suspended in that mirage
that only distance can make possible. It was time for the United
States to bolt its doors and sleep with the windows closed.

By now, Pau-Llosa and his contemporaries were beginning to
publish in major journals throughout the United States. Perhaps
some of these people are still trapped between their older country-
men and their North American counterparts, but a good number of
them have been quite successful. This success is due, in part, ˙ ⁻
their determination to not dwell on certain obstacles and limit
tions. It is not that the Cuban artist faces less discrimination, b
that he or she is able to transcend this. The result, in the poets' ca:
is poetry. Not political poetry. Not ethnic poetry. Not poetry
displacement. This is poetry that stands on its own and is so
recognized by editors, publishers, and readers around the world.

In his lectures, Pau-Llosa has frequently linked the Cuban
exile's commitment to art for its own sake to "pride in and lack of
anxiety over one's own cultural heritage." His analogy for Cuban
cultural continuity is that of a banquet in which different genera-
tions may be eating different foods with different utensils, but they
are doing so at the same table. "Cuban exile art and literature have
none of the angry and desperate attempts to restore what is pre-
sumed missing or what others have allegedly taken from them," he
has pointed out. "The feeling is that the imagination restores the
ravages of history by delighting in its own powers of creation."[21]

Those observing from the outside this commitment to continuity may see it as either futile or xenophobic. Most multilingual North Americans, however, believe that less fear of the outside world would lessen tensions between this country and the rest of the planet, and that learning other languages would break the ice and introduce us to other cultures. Carolyne Wright wonders if English-speaking Americans' disinterest in learning other languages is "one reason they are so offended by non-English speaking immigrants' seeming reluctance with respect to English."[22] What seems troubling to so many people is that Pau-Llosa's generation is not reluctant to learn English; on the contrary, it has mastered its adopted tongue. One would think the Anglo has nothing to fear from it. One would think this generation of Hispanic American writers woke up one morning and walked out the door and into the American Dream. But it's not that simple, is it? What is troubling to so many Anglos is that though the poetry is being written in English, the iconography is still foreign. It is one of those rare instances in which the melting pot theory has crystallized. All the myths, symbols, and values have seeped out of the earth through the roots, and they've been translated into the vernacular. Now what?

The English Only movement gained such momentum in Florida that the issue was put on the ballot in 1988. The proposition was worded in such complicated hyperbole that it seemed to be warning the voter that the alternative to English as official language would be Spanish taking over. The day of the election I spoke with an Anglo woman whose daughter had traveled throughout Western Europe. The woman defended multilingualism. She only objected, she said, to people who refuse to learn the languages of the countries where they find themselves when they leave their native land. This, I thought, seemed fair and logical enough. Then a third person who had been taking part in the conversation asked this woman if her daughter knew French, Spanish, German, Italian, etc. After all, the girl had traveled throughout Western Europe. No, the mother said. "Why learn any of those languages if everyone in the world speaks English?" The absurdity and the contradiction eluded her. That night I turned on the local news. The English Only coalition had won by a landslide.

Bread of the Imagined is a bridge between the xenophobic North America of the past and the multicultural country we have become but have trouble coming to terms with:

> Alone, a war had shoved me north.
> A boundary opened within me—
> on one side reaction to the world,
> on the other hope. The snowfall
> lost its shape then, passed over me,
> tried to include me
> in its white project of innocence.

For too many poets, the twentieth century ticks like a bomb. For Pau-Llosa, the end of the millennium is a heart beating with life. Our own tired hearts are aching for something solid, and yet, we still want the unexpected, the original, the words that leap like magical fish out of the page. We want to hear once again that innocent voice within us, the confident voice that tells us night after night that a sense of order prevails. Some mornings, listening to the news on the radio, we could swear we're living proof of the continental drift theory: just when we've learned to point to a certain border, the line curls up at the edge of the map, the country changes its name, and the entire population dissolves. Some nights, whole constellations fall into our open palms. We eat from our luminous hands. In times like these, an inarticulate hunger overpowers us, and we eat the bread of the imagined.

—Tampa, Florida/Exilio

October 1990

Notes

[1]Wendell Berry, *What Are People For?* (Berkeley: North Point Press, 1990), p. 73.

[2]Elías Miguel Muñoz, *Desde esta orilla: Poesía cubana del exilio* (Madrid: Editorial Betania, 1988), p. 23.

[3]Berry, pp. 89-90.

[4]Ricardo Pau-Llosa, "Identity and Variations: Cuban Visual Thinking in Exile Since 1959," in *Outside Cuba/Fuera de Cuba*, eds. Ileana Fuentes-Pérez, Graciella Cruz-Taura, and Ricardo Pau-Llosa (NJ/Miami: Rutgers/University of Miami, 1989), p. 41.

[5]Tom Wolfe, *The Painted Word* (NY: Bantam Books, 1980), p. 7.

[6]Susan Sontag, *On Photography* (NY: Dell Publishing Company, 1979), p. 6.

[7]Ricardo Pau-Llosa, from the introduction to *Paul Sierra: Recent Work*, catalog for the June 1990 show at Louis Newman Galleries, Beverly Hills.

[8]Ludwig Wittgenstein, quoted from "A Lecture on Ethics," *Philosophical Review*, 1965, pp. 3-12, in *The Enduring Questions*, ed. Melvin Rader (NY: Holt, Rinehart & Winston, 1976, 3rd ed.), pp. 640-647.

[9]Richard Hugo, *The Triggering Town* (NY: WW Norton, 1979), p. 12.

[10]Orlando Rodríguez Sardiñas, ed., *La última poesía cubana* (Madrid: Hispanova, 1973), pp. 30-31.

[11]On April 9, 1971, *Le Monde* published a letter in which some of the most renowned Western intellectuals warned Fidel Castro that the imprisonment of Heberto Padilla (following the publication of his book *Fuera del juego*) could only be detrimental to the Revolution. The letter was signed by over 30 Latin American and European writers, including Simone de Beauvoir, Julio Cortázar, Gabriel García Márquez, Jean-Paul Sartre, and Mario Vargas Llosa.

When the Cuban government forced Padilla to sign a retraction, the intellectual community wrote a second letter to Castro, expressing its anger and shame. The letter appeared, translated into Spanish, in the newspaper *Madrid* on May 21, 1971. Drafted in Paris on May 20, the letter's tone was much more direct than that of the first one. It exhorted Castro to keep Cuba free of the "cultural xenophobia and the repressive system imposed by Stalinism in Socialist countries. . . ." The number of signatures doubled and North Americans such as Susan Sontag joined the protest.

[12]Carolina Hospital, "Los Atrevidos," *Linden Lane Magazine* VI, 4 (October/December 1987), pp. 22-23.

[13]Ricardo Pau-Llosa, "Knot," from *Sorting Metaphors* (Tallahassee: Anhinga Press, 1983), p. 41.

[14]"Sorting Metaphors," *Sorting Metaphors*, p. 59-60.

[15]Carolina Hospital, "Pau-Llosa: A Poet Profile," *Linden Lane Magazine* VII, 1 (January/March 1988), p. 18.

[16]Ibid.

[17]W.H.D. Rouse, trans., *Great Dialogues of Plato* (NY: Signet, 1956), p. 399.

[18]Ibid.

[19]Joan Didion, *Miami* (NY: Simon and Schuster, 1987).

[20]See Note 12.

[21]Ricardo Pau-Llosa, from a lecture on Cuban art given at Hawk's Cay, Duck Key, Florida, July 20, 1990.

[22]Carolyne Wright, "English Revisited," *Before Columbus Review* 16 (May 16, 1989), p. 19.

References

Bernstein, Charles, ed. *The Politics of Poetic Form*. NY: Roof Books, 1990.

Bloom, Allan. *The Closing of the American Mind*. NY: Simon & Schuster, 1987.

Campbell, Joseph, with Bill Moyers, *The Power of Mythology*. NY: Doubleday, 1988.

Casal, Lourdes, ed. *El caso Padilla: Literatura y revolución en Cuba*. Miami/NY: Ediciones Universal/Ediciones Nueva Atlántida, 1972.

Cuadra, Angel. *Escritores en Cuba socialista*. Washington: La Fundación Nacional Cubano-Americana, 1986.

Hijuelos, Oscar. *The Mambo Kings Play Songs of Love*. Farrar, Straus, Giroux, 1989.

Hospital, Carolina, ed. *Cuban American Writers: Los Atrevidos*. Princeton: Ediciones Ellas/Linden Lane Press, 1988.

I

The Island of Mirrors

The Island of Mirrors

> "The objects we look at produce very
> perfect images at the back of our eyes."
> —Descartes, *Dioptric*

The dream where land
breaks like surf
cannot be dreamt.
Such a dream would pull
the anchor from the heart
and set the world adrift
like a plague ship,
the rats turning into words.

Take the dream,
the fertile dream of an eye,
and take a dead man's eye,
remove the membranes around it
(all this in your dream)
and replace the membrane
with eggshells. Hold
the eye in a light
tidal with images.
They will awaken on the shells.

Take the little world
of safety in places that bear us.
An island bore me, a land
filled with double mirrors,
so that it was no longer
an island but a space
memory resolves to leave us in
like an infant bundle.
The only real space
lives in a dead man's eye.

Orchids

for Luisa Richter

I overlook Caracas through gates of vine
braided with orchids. Like first snow,
in lumps their petals tilt in the hill-cleansed air.
They are dropped from heaven and fallen anywhere,
at our very feet if we could float
up the lianas or dance
upon the stream's moonlit glass.

Back home in winter I will see orchids at shows
wearing ribbons. Others will be drafted
to fight vulgarity's cause on a sequined breast.
Or in some residence I will happen on an orchid
posing in front of art like a museum guide
pointing at a painted cheek.
They will not signify their keeper's wish.
I will dream that the humming bird
has brought the monkey to nibble
on the mangos left on the terrace. He jolts
when I step from the curtain and races up the vines
tearing a hundred orchids in his panic to heaven.
Their petals glide to the forest floor like manna.

But here his terror is no catastrophe
for everywhere the orchid lives in naive abundance,
and what are a hundred losses to innocence?
They live as love should among us, their canopy
filtering the sun into a speckled light
that rhymes our flesh with the orchids'.
I stand in the terrace and the roots of clouds
dangle into my open hand
from which the monkey takes a ripe mango.
I cannot see myself in his eyes, only the world.

Edge of the Storm

A life may pass without
one having ever seen, not once,
a street halved by the border
of a storm, one side skull dry
and the other cloaked in a torrent.
Surely there are phenomena
which are both contained
and diffuse, clear in their emblems—
rain, thunder, lightning,
the leafy breeze before and after—
while imprecise in their boundaries.

I have seen the edges of many storms.
The first time on a street in Havana
along with other children holding out
hands into thick rain, caps brimming.
We pushed the group weakling into the rain
and we laughed to see him caged in water,
enclosed in what we had barely touched.
I thought of jumping in with others,
but the rain stopped and we scattered home.

Years later I saw the edge of a snowfall.
The brick houses dimmed as if inside
a paperweight souvenir blizzard.
Alone, a war had shoved me north.
A boundary opened within me—
on one side reaction to the world,
on the other hope. The snowfall
lost its shape then, passed over me,
tried to include me
in its white project of innocence.

Storm Chaser

He hunts the fear
descending cone
by radioed numbers
and leaves his car
to ponder the hard edge
of burnt cumuli
against the gold
sky, praying
for the turning point
to come down
like heaven's fingertip
to the pummeled ground.

The bright anvil
from afar has forged
the plain darkness,
has rained the ice
and fire, has spoken
the deafness of thunder
in the bony air.
The white towers
have simplified
into anger,
but not for the man
who enters
against the grain of flight.
For him the storm is
a pure thing
in its only language.

His binoculars
frame the stubborn
house dissolving,
and the cars that fold
like drought-crumpled beasts,
and the crops sown
like soldiers' blood.
He is the reaper

of the scorned harvest,
and he is here to celebrate
the perfect arrival
of a force.
And desires simply
its pondering
and record.

Nearby
a pool is the land's eye
watching wings at last
spiriting a body
into the sky.
He joins the pond's reflection
on the torn offering
drowned in distance.
The mind escapes
but guards itself to stay,
heeding the call to flee
by denying it.
The storm chaser
turns his eyes upon the dark promise
of a twister finally on the horizon.
Let others seek refuge from his dance.

Fly

On the red plastic chair—
dimpled like fat,
the opal of a fly
stares roundly at the world.

His eyes
split and sow
the earth
into themselves.
I eat a slice
of cold pizza which, too,
his diamond lens inhales
the way a promise fills
the belly of the poor.

His eyes equal the world,
all of it in them, all of it
the same, be it shit or banquet,
he finds it all attractive metal,
with neither lust nor patience.
A cloud's ghost passes,
and he darts from it
as if his own
lightning
could purge his fear
of smaller speeds.
My hand but for the swatting
could be the cloud,
an angel, manna falling.

My eyes—
who see like and if—
would starve him
in harvest Egypt.
The squandering son

has grown his eyes
to hunger for all.
Where all is appetite
not even God can play vulture.

Bones and Water

From below,
the anchored boats
are taut kites.
I free a coin
that glints toward the sand,
a broken butterfly.

Here and there clichés
of plants that lie
because they are animals.
Are the beasts the masters
of this place?

Bones betray them
everywhere,
a puzzle that says
to die is to be known dead.

The plants leave
neither bone nor ghost.
Their absent past
is a call to vanishing,
to the dignity of it.

A cut. Blood knows
finned shadows come quicker
than angels.

Exile

> "Un pájaro y otro ya no tiemblan."
> —*Lezama Lima*

Let these birds turn into circles,
holding themselves like so much gray,
and let them mean nothing
else than the knot of trajectories.
In the parks of another youth
those other birds trembled branches
into lines that broke the sky,
and from the breeze-drawn shadows
they sang as clouds of leaves
quivered like minnows.

Each bird was a heart in the great
green heart of the tree.
In those parks we would have melted
into the one song of a thousand
brown, dwarfed birds together
composing their gigantic call,
the harmony that guides and loves.
Then we would have made the hours pure
with the hand, the kiss, the word.

Key Biscayne

Between two coconut palms
we saw towers shattered
on the water's skin, novas
swallowed by Miami's scales.

Sipping Cointreau, we search
the bay for two kinds of refuge.
I am the fisher of metaphors
that bind the layered water
to bark and fronds.
Layers everywhere, see the squinting
condos and banks across the bay,
clothes and traffic, tiles,
patterns of which city and flesh are made.

You see better. If I had a camera, you say,
I'd shoot the base of the palm's crown. The spades
from which the fronds spring are smooth against
the knots and fibers surrounding them. It tells
me as much about the tree as about the world,
the city and us. A world of patterns that by sheer
number and intersection becomes a world of randomness.
It tells me that chaos is a blizzard of order,
and I stave it off by gazing at one thing
and its dignity reigning in my mind at that moment.

I test what I have learned from you later
at a red light. My pane is a drop lit sky.
I behold the simplest circles
of rain in a puddle, how two echoes
enter each other, become each other
yet stay two rings, not one.

Articles of Childhood

Two socks
hang from night's chair
like fruit in the hands
of a ghost. Shoes,
their tongues curled,
pronounce
the incense of sweat.

The ceiling hosts
my shadow
descending
on the child
far from the bed-drowned
parents. Tremble.
But I am anchored
by these fossil feet
dirty with life.
Night the scar

is now the child's dream,
my darkness lives.
A sweater on the wrinkled floor
is a torn hand
on a random shallow of beach.
From within the belly of a shell,
my half light shape has come.
It is, like mud, of two worlds,
continuous as fear.

He dreams
for three days
the snail clings,
a jewel
on the
rotting
laminaria
drifting.
He curls

into the
symmetry
of birth.

Together we become
the horizon
of obscene skin—
shell, glove.
Man the tortoise
abandons earth's night
for the sea.

II

Fog's Edge

Fog's Edge

A great color need not be ambiguous
as it overtakes farms, fences, animals
on the plateau. It can leave
things out there where details glisten—
the grass swords,
the clod-crumpled paths—
or it can embrace the daily earth
in its white arrivals.

All fogs have a white mind,
and so they think the house,
the knightless horses,
the fading mountains
are bronze, green, zinc
aberrations all yearning
to drink its white fire.
To be dissolved,
enclosed, to free one's fragments
to space and vapor is not
to lose oneself, thinks the house
as the fog comes over it
dislodging it like a shell
it anchored yesterday
on a punctual shore.

To be dissolved, thinks the horse,
is to know the highest freedom of the race,
the heart-splintering gallop
whose rider is time.
To melt away in fog's crucible,
thinks the earth, is to break
its endless chore
of holding back the unfinished
angers of lava and steam.
When the fog comes the earth knows
its rocks will float like spores
and the lace of its leaves will come undone.

The Flight of the Labyrinth Maker's Son

My plowman's shoulder,
Brueghel notes, is blind
to the drowned wings.
But my deaf back
is far from mute, knows
Icarus better than God.
He flew for himself
who falls for others.

Why waste a glance, a fist?
Had his toes grazed the grass tips,
and his bronze shadow haloed
the soles' arrival, would he
embrace me as his free brother?

At court men like Icarus wreathe
the tyrant with laughter.
My laurels are sweat.
Their king who takes
my crops for history
has turned my teeth
into a tongue's cage.
They only visit what I endure,
in dreams and words they sell me.

As I thirsted, Icarus toasted in my name.
Drink now, Icarus, drink.
The king and the plowman raise
their cups to you. Be consoled, Icarus.
Only the Minotaur ignores you.

Aquarium

This bar is an aquarium
with an aquarium for a heart.
A fish like a violet eye
stares from the calcium lid
of a shell, one of many
white strewn halves,
familiar perimeters
of their alien makers.

The fish esses
up the tapering tail
of a conch and through
the harp of bubbles
urgently obeying
an inverted gravity—
the violent melody
of a spectral extreme.

It is nothing
but the role I assign to it,
an extreme myself amid
the grunting maneuvers
of bar chatter. I am quiet
and let my thoughts swirl
through genies of cigar smoke
uncorked from my mouth.
A wish, master, a wish:
to be fish-like
in a fluid world.

The tank has other citizens,
striped prisoners of commonness,
blue-collared snails
filling the panes with algicide.
Only one violet eye
looks at this from within,
and I insist he be the startled
mind, heavy with witnessing,

torn and hiding in the gaudy
fill of shells and unswayed
plastic laminaria.

He doesn't scare
when his reflection
fictions on the glass
as do the others.
He scares, rather, at their scaring
and enters a nostalgia
he has gardened since birth.
A trite angling of the body
over a bar, brandy glass
and cigar are only the passports
to unreconciled coexistence
with vulgar passings.

The Burial of the Elephant at Cremona

Its body fills
the small piazza with shadows
only clouds were thought to make.
Its parenthetical trunk and cries
kept many at home, shuttered
with rosaries, though most filled
the streets and rooftops to gaze
at their emperor's gift
to Cremona. But the gift died
in three days and the king
was off to Bologna with his panthers,
hawks and giraffes.

The priest, who had sermoned us
on the king's evil, sprinkled holy water
on the vast gray flanks,
the walls of elephant, praying
for a horde of vultures to descend
and eat the carcass down to the light
bones we could all carry on our own.
The vultures never came, not one,
and the smell of elephant death
reached every corner of Cremona.

Our engineers grudgingly measured
the carcass from afar, calculating
size by length of shadows at dusk.
Only a few penitents, eyes white
and backs lined with whipmarks,
came to chant at the beast's side,
their voices and ivory flames
hovering over the abandoned
piazza. As they climbed the body
and chanted litanies, a starless
half-moon descended above them.
Blocks away in our tavern
we could hear their elaborate

cries, the sandals against
the granite and stone of the square.

Finally, it was posted that all of us
had to remove the carcass and bury it.
Since no one came, the priest perhaps,
or relic traders, or the mayor, or all
of them said the bones would turn to ivory
after the beast was buried a month
and unearthed under a full moon.
Noted Arabic scholars confirmed this,
and the Romans were said to have made
fortunes from the bones of Hannibal's
war beasts. Things would change.

But who would dare touch
the beast, climb the wrinkled
gray declines of rotting flesh,
or axe through the carcass
and carry it off in pieces to its grave,
this silver beast of the moon,
as the rasp of shovels forges
the crater and the morning cumuli
mushroom on the horizon.

The Beauty of Treason

With death at hand,
a conclusion: let the poem—
ignoble, frightened thing—
be thrown into the fire.
The emperor guessed something else
had moved him through the tongue,
beyond the specifics of feeling,
the quarters of thought, the valor.
"Through fear and into love,"
said the emperor, clearing his throat,
"the future drove your hand,
and love, lying in some to be,
said write and I'll possess you,
untrembling, O bird wing!"

Moved, the poet spared the text and died.
He was from another country,
ambassador, discreet, often in love.
He had learned the music of the court
and found it better than that of his own
land, which he was now forgetting.
In the end, he had lived
most of his life at the court,
happy to confuse his dreams for theirs.
In his poem his native land lived with such
precision that the emperor's generals
had much use of it during the conquest.

Point Blank—The Footbridge

Beneath her soles the wooden sounds
tried to match the ladder of lines,
one closer to the next, her eyes
extended before her infinitely.
The assigned project seemed hard enough
to be simple—dispense with causes
so that the world of the eye
lifts pure like a canvas and
that of the ear a state in which
all noises share.
The sleeping wall of narrow waters
beneath her like a mirror in an attic,
a rink of dust where no lights dance.
This is the way, she spoke to herself.
And avoiding them, a thought came
descending on the back of a hibiscus,
which is to say, a metaphor.

The flower fell before her like a glove,
and in her Way it was a form like any other.
There is no weight in the eye, and had this
been a stone would it not have fallen
like a flower that falls like a glove?
Her heart withdrew into its happiness.
At last no thing was more
than any other, no power lived,
no appetite disguised dominion as need.
The flower would fall
through its brother, the blue form
of the sky, and make a simple sound in her heart—
that other form, that stone waiting to fall.

She shed the simple tears of such occasions
and started home to her jealous husband,
the emperor's closest advisor,
a genius of suspicions. Unbeknownst
to her, on the beach that day
her teacher had died in contemplation

when an osprey dropped a turtle on his head.
When she arrived the husband
read her unfaithful tears.
He had her beheaded in the morning.

Lessons at Lake Lanier

for the Molinas

By the man-made lake, the seeming dead
trees guard winter's end with a metaphor:

Naked and more broken than detected lies,
the branches are the veins of clouds.
Morning rains have rewritten the lake's
translucency. The bronze two ducks traverse
might have been glass.

From the terrace of a weekend
retreat I patrol reckless thoughts.
My eye paints the other guests
in the taut spaces between trunks.
Nature, artifice?
Miles somewhere, a dam conjures
lightning from this still life.

By the shore two boys enter gestures
I cannot read, a dance that shatters
autumn shrapnel. On the drive into the city,
they told me how they battled
the ogres of boredom, stumps
were heads of buried enemies, and eddies
the ineffable speech of a neutral spirit.
The squirrels were our messengers,
but the birds quivered with hate for our cause.
A grateful princess watched us
sharpen our swords with blood.
The lake was the acid eye of a giant
cursed to disbelieve everything it sees.
Into it the last villains were hurled.

I was the bloodless winter,
the music beneath each step.

Charles V, Honeymoon in Seville

It would be years before the emperor would remember,
astride the corpses of Turks in Vienna,
to think it strange how on the first
twilight of his marriage he would gaze upon a street
of nippled oranges and feel like a bird
on a branch in vast paradise.

Naked on his balcony, he watched a hundred gypsies
getting ready for the night. Not one
orange had been plundered, a miracle,
he thought, until his bride
propped herself on a pillow and spat
into the silver tray, "Acid! These oranges
are only good for marmalade." She gaped
at her fingers as if they were dripping blood.

His sudden turn toward her startled
the birds in what had been the ablution fountain
in the mosque courtyard, el Patio de los Naranjos.
It was a perfect square grided with orange trees,
infinite pillars, Allah's echo. In its center
the fountain bloomed, the lotus genesis of a sphere.
The emperor would recall it when his architect raised
the round courtyard of his palace next to the Alhambra
like a host. He had planned to live with Isabel
above Granada. When she died he planned to just endure
there, far from the bloods and maps of faith,
beside a hushed labyrinth of African pleasure.

How unlike he was now to the king Titian painted
on his steed advancing like the sun
onto victory and horizons.
From the monk's table he takes a bitter orange,
and it is no longer the planet resting
on his fingertips. Nor is it
the circle entwined in a square
that reconciles heaven and earth.

It is the fruit which love must leave unconquered.
On bundled rags the gypsies dream
the oranges split like wine skins
and wash them in gold.

Classroom, Bulletin Board

Across the sand, ghosts of white writings
are about to dissipate. Echoes of forms
and letters—S, 4, T, DR—
loop like the blurred trails of a snake.
I ponder this desert standing
in a kind of sky, perpendicular
to the aluminum framed expanse,
message naked. Hovering in the purest
vertical, I see two rectangles
on the upper right of shadow darkened grains
and another on the left. Between them
a dance of white losses that map
the dialogue between minimal masks.

The bottom flank of the bulletin board
is peopled with graffiti rising
onto the ochre space from the desks below.
More visible than the white blurrings,
the ink doodlings denote even greater
transience, the reckless fruit of passing.
Their darkness is ironic here against
the ochre and beneath the white and the masks.
Like shattered tattoos which have been
thrown up on shore, seaweed shrapnel,
their tumblings utter an absolute surface.

The empty board begins to look
like an island assailed at its edges
by a human sea. And what of us,
more than islands, planets to countless
mites and organisms fettered to our hairs
and the cracked trenches of our flesh,
to eyelash, nail and lip?
Do our countless citizens write their lives
upon us, unread? What calamitous myths
might they conjure if they had the bones

of a mind each time we plunge into the sea
or make love or scratch unthinkingly away
the invisible walking we sometimes sense
across this land of skin?

Dart

That day the losing was not like
the breeze through the hiding grasses,
nor the smells of freshly killed
gazelle, their young bellies
opened like red pages.

A shot and I awoke
with a collar and an ear tag.
Someone, for whom I am only
a weight and a length, maps
my life and calls me species.

The dart made me dream what I cannot recall.
For moments I was both panther and warden.
I sink slowly into each dusk like a hippo
wading into mud silvers. He knows
the air of the world is hung ripe
with patient stars and trees.
What I forget I swim in again each night.

After the dream I looked up
and saw the ground, a constellation
of rocks and weeds, but the gazelle
I had killed in the dream was gone
and the panther I had weighed was gone.

When I mate, kill, eat,
wander the savannah like breath,
or lengthen my body on a branch to sleep
with my legs dangling like fruit,
I know that reliving spares remembering.
I am others, I died, and now I get on with it.

III

The Room

The Room

after the photographs of Silvia Lizama

Ignore the ruins of toys, the animal
curves of wires and their live
shadows, the doors bleeding light.
These windows belong to no idea.
This room your steps have brought
you to is a feeling.

There is no one here,
only your absence witnesses
the lamp's glowing cones
on the detachment of papered walls.
Think nothing,
a secret season is in residence.
The green whose biography the sea
must write cannot be read here.

You have eaten the bread of the imagined,
and you are ready to leave.
Go quietly, vanish like a scarf
the unreined wind has sunk into a puddle.
They will not believe you when you tell them
a color can be the blood of a time.

Brooms

after the photograph by Mario Algaze

Bristling with usefulness
and the coarse blues and textures
of new things, the brooms recline
against wall, grating, door, and counter.
This bouquet of brooms will fall apart
that one by one they might claim
the territory of some function
in each house on the village street.
They yearn, though you would never
detect it seeing them in easy bundles
at the bodega, to be alone,
in time ragged, dirty, balding,
their hearts of straw broken.
They spy a housewife who walks
past them and would bend toward her
like orphic branches. At night,
when the owner's gone and dust
and rats have their say in the cobalt air,
they dream of those old brooms
that will not die in their closets,
the favorite brooms of those housewives
whose blistered habits have written themselves
on the worn, paintless sticks.
So long as the old brooms hold out,
these brooms at the bodega must spend
their dreams together, bound by a string
and that strange hatred which only beings
waiting for their destiny can breed.

The Intruder

after the painting by Julio Larraz

He comes amid the light of apples,
the window's dusk and the marble curtains.
Though slightly, he moves
the faces fruit and cloth turn
to the lace angles of morning.

No new order results
as he allows his shadow
to fall like a peel
among the elements of beauty.

A simple beast, a monkey
in a still life, and yet his acts
are part of the scene's
incantatory, ambiguous praise
of thereness and frailty.

Unlike a kiss or a comet,
he vanishes imperfectly—
like a fist blossoming,
a city blurring into guardian sands,
or the hate of a woman.

Century of Light

Above, the loins and backs
of a harem bath.
Huge, pink, anatomical
clouds wrinkle into gray
or fan into the spectrum
crash of a wave. The breast
of a sail sundials the Gulf Stream.

The bellied ship knows
what moves the waves
and paints the sky
is not number or god.
A sound is heard, desire.
It is like falling coins
and breath at once,
rigging and linen on course.

A dorsal arc by compass drawn
rolls upward. The leaden
mottled flank swallows
a swimmer or junk and dives
with the terse flap of its hourglass tail.
It sinks through impasto waves
to festooned depths where gold-leaf
seraphs blast their mute horns.

Battlefields

after the paintings of Alejandro
Obregón and Antonio Amaral

In the myth of conflict, doubt sustains.
The winner, disguised in calculations,
trembles before the prey. For this
such things as hovering were invented.
The incantatory pause of wings
held by the ghost hand of warm air
haunts all the silences of weight
until a sure folding drops them
along a hypotenuse to the kill.
The rabbit on the ground is the vertex
in a geometry he ignores,
until her claws hoist him
through parabolas of desert air
bringing meat to the hungry.

Can an image surrender?
In fact, it can do nothing else
but dwell in some order to which matter
arrives, e.g., circles coined
from the fruit's ripe innocence.
Five silver prongs surface
on the banana's skin
like suns tearing through morning mist.
Flayed, she reclines on the dessert dish,
an open parenthesis
closed by her porcelain shadow.
The waiting is soon over
as the knife and fork hover.
"Things matter or they don't matter,"
says one guest. "Nothing
is so simple," retorts another.
The knife plunges and the fork hoists
the circles to their chemical apotheosis.
"A martyr," says the host,
"is always consoled
by the fables of consummation."

The Inventors

The van's painted diver aims his speargun
at a busful of tourists, sunglassed as none
of our own. The dark lines of his mask
and gear against the van's too bright blue
and green, an unreal fish bubbles
expectantly for his death, turns left
at 27th Avenue and brakes
too abruptly at every tide
of traffic and red lights. The driver
sips often from a paper bag, the smell
of his catch reaching us, bass and trout
no doubt, and shrimp that flock to lights
hung over boatsides on the bay,
the nets efficiently reaping the dumb
phototropic crustaceans,
$7.89 a pound and rising
like the moon and those first stars
that come unnoticed.
That group on the left
seems to stand for something,
the bright red one a shoulder,
three forming a belt at the center,
the great back is a great silence.
Pursuing and pursued, a lover punished,
let us say a giant buried in the sky
by bright passion, now a catch of glass
and pondered lines. His great arm
and club, he hears the quantum
cry of space that moves him, his face
whitens into novas of anger.
As darkness is his prey, our fish scare
more brightly among the papyrus reeds.
At last our killing has a name,
a guardian, a calendar.

Caryatides

> "Their slavery was an eternal warning. Insult crushed them. They seemed to pay a penalty for their fellow citizens."
> —Vitruvius, *On Architecture*

They are things we learn from,
each one the patient shadow of the others,
standing, awed, painless.
They survived to suffer
their city's politics. Victory
was not in their just stars,
their men slaughtered, Persia
routed. Caria, the stone sin
of your women has taught us
to live the life of loyal flesh.

A porch of maidens,
each burdened sibilant
could speak her stony guilt
and make us cry, like drama,
but all we see are ordered knees
bent to some Attic symmetry.
One, whose drapery has yellowed,
is a necessary counterfeit.
A young architect cannot help
but flash his camera at her breasts.
He speaks of numbers and ignores
the sudden rage
that moved golden Athens to genocide
and made her sculptors fix in stone
the lessons of innocence and poise.

White Water

after the painting by Paul Sierra

Do not hate the flood.
Revel in the song of water
churned whiter than ghosts.
Do not hate the stallion
waves bursting free.

A year ago the flood begins,
calm as an old thought, with a harvest
of snow in the mountains. The reeded banks
give, the boulder tilts, the oak
surrenders, then the house
folds like a fan and the road melts,
the herd is swallowed as if by memory.
The raft a leaf in the world thick torrent.

In the painting, the houses and trees
are not shattered or drowned but gathered
and laid, like offerings,
at the feet of blind pillars.

Above, a bridge where a traveler
has gazed at the moon, then at the neat wreckage,
then at the moon, then at a bronze coin
in his right palm. He is sure now
that the world is the creaking
planks under his naked soles
because the bridge
is precisely halfway between the house
he thinks must be torn and the moon.

Do not hate this traveler,
you who a thousand deaf times have walked
past the poetry of beggars
and the thunder of brushstroke.

Minimalism

At the count of three
you will think
of nothing
else but this poem,
of nothing
else but its taut
images all of which
you have met before but casually.
After you have accepted
the direct forms
these images take
and realize it is their abstractness
and not their place in the world
which makes them yours,
you will have two options:
awaken if you understood the exercise,
or if you didn't—become
"one with these forms,"
as they say.

Smoke

for Fernando Luis (1932-1983)

Slowly advancing, iron and steam,
over tracks laid expressly
for your entry into dark forests,
Life slammed you shut
like a book.

The citizens of your mind were stunned
to see you stumble in mid-life.
In reverence, they sank
deeper into their brothel
intrigues. In unison they lit
cigarettes—incense of the mundane—
to fill the soul's room
with the wreckage of breath.

You trained them to ignore the infinite,
hoard and polish the shrapnel.
You painted rats like popes, and whores
as if they meant something.
A man can lose his teeth
laughing in a nightmare.

Nude Man Bending into a Mirror

after the painting by Arnaldo
Roche-Rabell

Of course his face is different
from this angle, the shoulders and back
zooming behind the face to the sunset or ceiling.
When he looks up into mirrors
in elevators the sun sets on the floor,
his hair and features sink
and his shoe tips stick out
of his chin, or is it his belly?

Now the cheeks are pulled toward the pane
and the eyes marble and droop
into the mirror, preparing to dive.
In its water he is as deaf
as the water he pulls himself from.

No one knows this man
in this way, and this is his own
first try at bending down naked
into the goblet-shaped mirror
he holds in the right hand,
his buttocks nudging
the carved corner of a table.
Above the table a painting
full of symbols of things
he paints with:
palette, spatula, fork and blade.

The man is on fire
in the picture of himself
looking down into the mirror
that is sucking him into the water.
I say he is on fire—
just look at the yellows
and oranges, and the reds,
and all around him the darkness,
just as it is with fire, the darkness.

The man does not hear me
because his left hand
is blocking the mirror.
Icicles of wet hair like
cavern rocks crash
into the pane, or might.
But he cannot eclipse the lip
of the table or its lion leg
which comes down between his legs
and which he can see behind him
in the mirror, O if only he looked.

The sharpened symbols and the table
come upon him like panthers rising
from a dart's dream. The flesh
imagines, the flesh holds mirrors
to eyes that swim out to sea
and mark a horizon in each stroke
as the frames in a movie
mark the destinies of light.
The eyes never return,
not even to embrace a forgiven son.

IV

Swirling Lines

Ladder

shore's book of waves,
the equal equal signs of a map,
clouds like roots, ruler,
days, seeds, air's labyrinth of lungs,
DNA, films, piecing together
the broken, pi, ice, inflation,
the tread mill what's that again,
forgive me, then again
then again, virus and commas, dial tones,
torpedo bubbles, harp strings, the silent
hull drowning, the anchor on its deck
finally art, a forest between two trunks,
the last buck on 17 red,
loved, the counterfeit
calendar with some wrong dates, surely
a step, then another, on the wobbly rungs
is not entirely like snow
falling to a warm earth.

What Is a Face?

Both process and thing,
like a clock, landscape, or building,
it is even the obvious:
emblem, key, curtain, glove,
but is more like a flower,
both process and thing,
a pattern, formula, chain, question,
an arena, an organism,
an absence like a well,
the promise of an absence
like a box, it is a hinge,
and it can be a piano or violin
for these are not played with hands.
A face does not belong in a hand.
It is not a mask

despite the rumors.
A face is a shell (as in egg and tortoise)
and a conch which is another kind
of window or door, a text
be it poem, letter, or
code scrambler or book, a map
and a prism, but it is not a mirror.
It is not a candle or a haystack
for some things that are processes
are not faces. It is not a concept
like energy, sound, distance, or thought,
it is not a set of tracks on the beach,
nor a tile floor, but it is a carpet,
and it is a fish and a brushstroke.

A face is a body, but it is not
any one of its parts, neither is it
an eye, a nose, or a mouth. It is a
fist for this is not part of a body
but a facing of one part of the body
toward something like a wing or a motor
both of which are also faces, both

of which are things and processes.
A face is a net, a fruit, an astrolabe,
a funnel, but neither
a storm nor a season, and not jewelry
unless it is a watch or a necklace.
It is not a paperweight or bookends.
It is not a car, plane, or train
(although it could be a train at times).
On the prow of a ship it is uneasy.

It is never food, but it is recipes
and a table set for five or three or one.
Smoke is a face provided it swirls
from a resting cigarette.
A face is a hearth, however, and it is a napkin.
It is not a flag or money or a roll
of uncut fabric, not cutting utensils,
not a kite or a ballroom, but a face
is a picture of a dog on a frail, long
leash where the master's hand is out of the picture.
A face is a storm-felled branch,
and any kind of clothes especially armor
and lace, and a postcard, but it can never be
punctuation or anything determined by chance
like the paths of wind-blown newspapers.

Acceleration

That smudge ahead, oil
on the road's shrinking distance,
turns into a hole that steering might
consider or braking, to a blood
marbled dog opening like pages,
to a tire or rag clump
knotting into a bum's body
that is a box, wet
cardboard I pass over like wind
and see in my mirror as it regains
its human folds, a soldier
tiring of orders and seasons,
becoming a wound, a crater
in plains where armies dissolve
like speech, abandoned
Moscow on the new year's map
but a smudge now.

66

Ricardo Pau-Llosa

A Hingeless Box

The man without gloves
has tried to keep our promises.

A woman without words
has tried to look speechless.

Where is the bird whose flight
everyone had learned by heart?

The well is to shadow
what the basket is to bread.

In the life of a drop
a leaf is a chapel.

One sends a rebel to the park
for air and water, and one hopes.

Freedom as Etymology

We start somewhere with a feeling
and drop to the pond floor, inventing
line, readying our smoothness.
Remember the skin of the lake,
how it haloed with our intrusion?
At that moment the day-filled cypress,
the rusty verb of toads, and the cat-tail
metronomes were concentric witnesses
to the crown of splash.

Then erasings were born,
the last whisper of arc reached
the deaf shore, and on the swallowed
bread of stone mold grew and stillness.
Dozing in the archive of nature,
we became denotation—
words in God's sentences.
Leaves, our boundaries, came to mean us.
And the stone became word,
and from a mouth of clouds
another man is falling
into the lexicon of living.

Abundance

The boy will find no way
that is his own among the green
lights shooting from the pool
or the sun weavings
of the gold dust bees.
Sarah, the shepherd in heat,
has eaten one and the others descend
to exile us from the mottled pool chairs
beneath the flagrant trees.

At 18 my boy goes for broke by turns
I uphold, less father than audience
to his meanderings. He yawns
his next career and I dance
the phone circuits into nets
of cronies and sleep-buried debts.

Next morning, an architect no longer,
my boy yearns for agriculture or NASA
for surely there is just omen
in the breeze orbits of avocados
above his daily laps.
He rises from the pool's opal
like a silver seal and grins.
Dad, couldn't I be later something
and not now that the guys will come to throw
a while soon and I have a date later?
Of course, son. I understand

petting Sarah who tries to slink
past me and the servant to a neighbor's male.
Stay! and she becomes a stone
at my feet and waits
for my order to drown
against the cloudy statues by the pool
or in my cordless chatter in the sun.
Innocently she climbs
through widening stretches

like rungs, until she can turn
her sleepy jaws my way to check
if it is safe to dart at last
to the hole she dug beneath the fence.

Trees and Transformations

Green is the structure
that in the brain of clouds
unfurls its branches.
In clusters the avocados grow
still after the jay's spring
and its buoyant echo
of leaf and twig are hushed
by the breeze,
another page in the syntax of summer.
Is not a season a language
overgrown with unthought
propulsions?

The tree greens, flowers, and fruits—
a lesson too perfect to risk losing
in the vortex of origins,
although it is creation itself
that this rote harmony proclaims.
Walk beneath its mottled shadow
and think the tree holds you
like a wordless memorial of flesh
in the easy heat of backyards.

The wind jolts an avocado to the ground,
a bomb that thumps on the unhurt grass
its mime of the old shatterings.
If laid on its side like the horizon
of a bleached grammar,
the trajectory of the falling fruit
would have at one end Galileo
and at the other Dresden.
This fruit could be a heart,
if hearts were green.

The Metaphor of Menace

Soon the poems in the voices will stop.
They will not march down
from a heaven of absence
like Vallejo's rain
and forget themselves into the earth,
leaving only a stone of voices behind.
Instead, they will come into the office.
After the two smiles shake hands,
they will sit down and say nothing.
They will learn to leave.
But if they decide to stay,
they will have to share hate's room
(they know those rumors—that hate
is like an amber fist),
and they don't want to bother with it.
After they have left, we can talk.

Little Dog

They are happy
and I am a dog.
They eat at the table
which my breath holds up.

If I don't blink or breathe,
the table will dip
and more than crumbs will roll
into my mouth.

"You, I did not come for you,"
says the honored guest, to me.
To me? They never called you
"family." I helped them
wait for You.

Already, he runs the place,
and I bark. "Out!" they all say.
"Out"—a whip and a curse.
I stop breathing but the table
does not fall and the house
is unmoved and for once the wind
outside is not stirred by my tail.

I bark again, now among torn leaves.
We had a deal! So, who isn't a son
of a bitch? I bark and bark.
I gave you my best fleas!

I am too tired to rebel
and too smart to be agape.
I bark to con him. If he comes out
and kicks me or yells, then I'll know
we had something once.

Now I know what being sick as a dog means.
I know the difference between heal and heel.
At least tell me the deal's off! Bark, bark.
Stay with the trees,
at least they smell like me.

Seals

Like gloves stacked on a shelf
then dropped, the seals arc
the lead beach. All thumbs,
their barks climb the stark
cliff walls to reach us, broken,
a code no attention could sew.
No gesture moves them, except
the light twitch of loud heads
we know for sure dispatch
these sounds up the funneling bluffs
toward our viewpoint.

They are in season, like dark
fruit opportunely plump.
And yet they are rare.
Past a dozen viewing points
no sign of them till now, although
a mile ago we stared at a seal-like rock
until waves failed
to awaken it more than once,
and then we called it a rock for sure.

The certainty of the nameless lies
everywhere. Each rock, leaf, and beast
has a name we ignore, despite the park signs
that conjure silhouettes of poison oak
or breaching whales. We are from the city
and in love, and so we find
in this terrain the heart's echo,
where knowledge is too fast for names.
There feeling dips into the torn mantels of foam,
half woman and half fish, the sea lion
which deceived the Pinta's sailors.
I call them seals. The heart seals.
And as it does, it binds nothing.

Foreign Language

Every object is a room
you walk words into.
Take an apple, its windows peeling.
In your hands the apple's
door opens a crack
and the words barge through
like salesmen confident of a kill.
The gerund opens the mail,
the verb's hands rumble through
the refrigerator, an adverb
caresses the daughter's knee,
the noun, its feet on the sofa,
says everything is as it should be.
Teeth tear through the walls of the apple
like a plane crashing in the suburbs.
The mouth is full of a wet white word
you can't pronounce, a pronoun
reading the newspaper in the living room.
When you bit, you never knew what hit you.

Enclosures and Expirations

The wing's edge like the hand's,
parenthesis, calendar pages,
gates, shutters, bow ties,
the frayed turning into thread,
foreclosures, the slammed
door of a book, hairs
of the farthest root, amens,
?, the muted knock
of the ripe avocado's seed,
a fly's wingblur, nails
quirking as they enter
a magnet's range, chalk
ghosts of words on the board
like x-rays or tide-written sand,
the banyan canopy as dominion
and its shadow as map, the name
you recall only to forget again,
wall, doorframe, stretcher,
light's last stop in a spectrum,
line written, line drawn,
line beneath a column of numbers,
dead phone line, the cancelled check,
rhyme, music beginning to end,
a body's round apex in the hammock's triangle,
billiard balls set, the deer in the viewfinder,
suddenly understanding,
eclipse.

Swirling Lines

A brain, a tree heart,
the cellular meltings
of a galaxy, a fly's wing,
a torpedo's bubbly void,
a moiré dress shifting,
leaf, ear, onion, fist,
blood's canopy, rolled newspaper,
a knot of hair, a dozing
cat-o'-nine-tails, a ring
of cigar ash, grasses
on the river, a face diluted
on a concave, marble's calcium strings,
a snake nest, an astrolabe,
smoke writing or clenching,
a pineapple's crown, estuary
sand settling like pastry shells,
run-on opalescences, hamburger,
the acrobatics of streaks on glass,
geology's veils, a rippling pond,
a disemboweled wire, a bowl of pasta,
a peacock feather, cloud fronds,
the citadel of a car engine,
a star-of-Bethlehem, a bouquet
of cathodes and filaments,
squid embracing, genes,
an agate word, combed sand,
the lace of oil on water,
plywood, a terraced slope,
the penmanship of dance,
watermarks, a vortex of moss,
the ways of meaning, wet fur,
fire's filigree, a plowman's world,
an artichoke halved, a nautilus echo,
a deck of handkerchiefs arching
like papyrus heads, the mother-of-pearl
undulations of a porch screen,
brushstrokes, climate mapped

from a satellite, a labyrinth,
this thumb against the pane—
the face of touch—
on the first morning of spring.